EDGE
BOOKS

DRAWING COOL STUFF

HOW TO DRAW

# AMAZING
# MOTORCYCLES

by Aaron Sautter

illustrated by Tod Smith

Capstone
press

Mankato, Minnesota

Edge Books are published by Capstone Press,
151 Good Counsel Drive, P.O. Box 669, Mankato, Minnesota 56002.
www.capstonepress.com

*Library of Congress Cataloging-in-Publication Data*
Sautter, Aaron.
    How to draw amazing motorcycles / by Aaron Sautter ; illustrated by Tod Smith.
    p. cm.—(Edge books. Drawing cool stuff)
    Includes bibliographical references and index.
    Summary; "Lively text and fun illustrations describe how to draw amazing
motorcycles"—Provided by publisher.
    ISBN–13: 978-1-4296-0073-6 (hardcover)
    ISBN–10: 1-4296-0073-X (hardcover)
    1. Motorcycles in art—Juvenile literature. 2. Drawing—Technique—Juvenile
literature. I. Smith, Tod. II. Title. III. Series.
NC825.M66S28 2008
743'.896292275—dc22                                             2007003409

**Editorial Credits**
Jason Knudson, designer

1 2 3 4 5 6 12 11 10 09 08 07

# TABLE OF CONTENTS

# WELCOME!

You probably picked this book because you love motorcycles. Or maybe you picked it because you like to draw. Whatever the reason, get ready to dive into the world of amazing motorcycles!

Big, small, fast, or slow, motorcycles are a fun way to get around. Motorcycles come in many amazing shapes and sizes. From classic 1930s models with sidecars to today's fast racers, many people love riding them.

This book is just a starting point. Once you've learned how to draw the different motorcycles in this book, you can start drawing your own. Let your imagination run wild, and see what sorts of fantastic machines you can create!

# To get started, you'll need some supplies:

1. First you'll need drawing paper. Any type of blank, unlined paper will do.

2. Pencils are the easiest to use for your drawing projects. Make sure you have plenty of them.

3. You have to keep your pencils sharp to make clean lines. Keep a pencil sharpener close by. You'll use it a lot.

4. As you practice drawing, you'll need a good eraser. Pencil erasers wear out very fast. Get a rubber or kneaded eraser. You'll be glad you did.

5. When your drawing is finished, you can trace over it with a black ink pen or thin felt-tip marker. The dark lines will really make your work stand out.

6. If you decide to color your drawings, colored pencils and markers usually work best. You can also use colored pencils to shade your drawings and make them more lifelike.

# CLASSIC CHOPPER

Choppers have low seats, high handlebars, and extra-long front suspensions. People like them for their unique look and feel. Chopper fans love to customize their bikes with lots of chrome and special paint details.

After drawing this bike, try it again using your own cool designs!

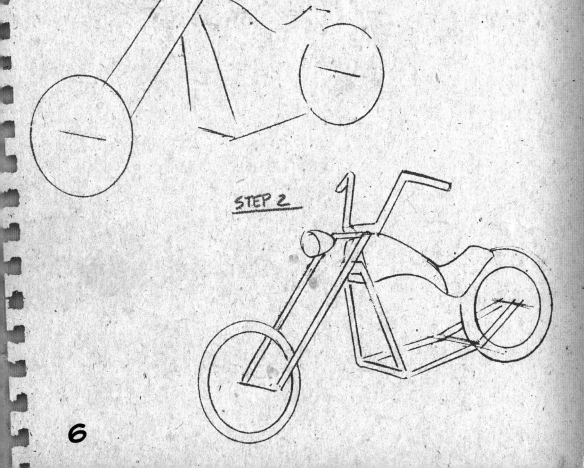

STEP 1

STEP 2

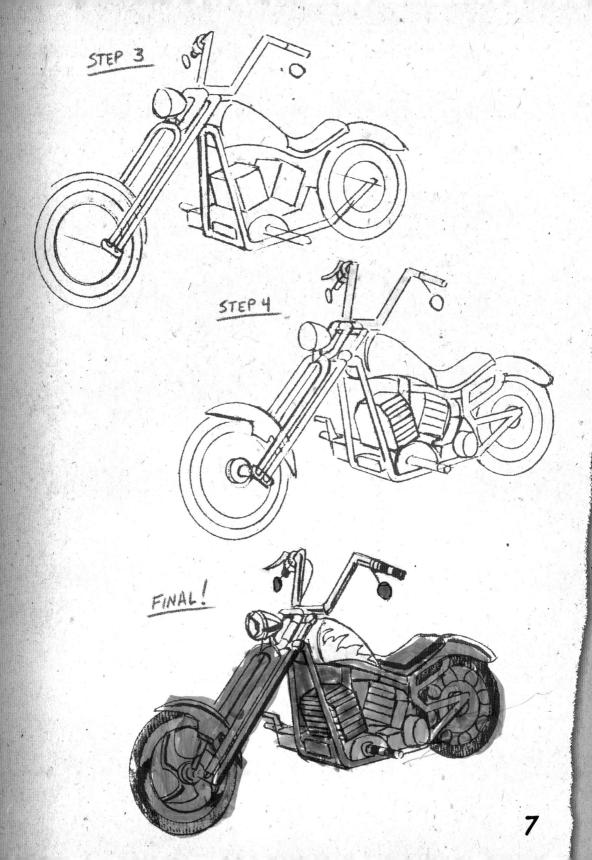

STEP 3

STEP 4

FINAL!

7

# THE HOG

The Hog is often given credit for making motorcycles popular. Its simple design, powerful engine, and easy handling make it perfect for both rookies and experienced drivers alike. Hop on—let's go for a ride!

When you're done drawing this bike, try it again going down the open road.

STEP 1

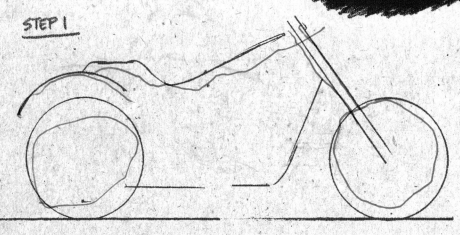

STEP 2

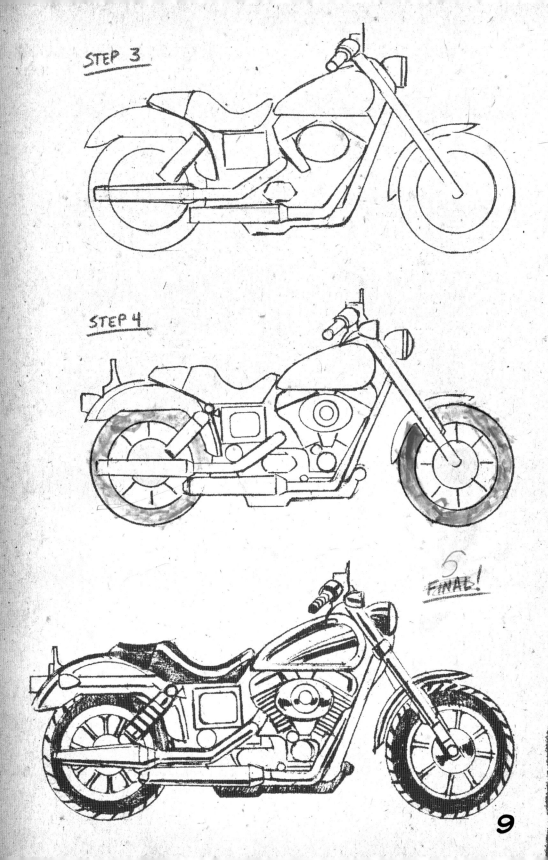

STEP 3

STEP 4

5
FINAL!

9

# THE ROCKET-EX3

For all-out speed on the open road, nothing beats the Rocket-EX3. This sleek bike has the most powerful non-racing engine available. It can go from 0 to 60 miles per hour in just 3.02 seconds!

To show this bike's speed, try adding flat lines flying out behind it to make a blur effect.

**STEP 1**

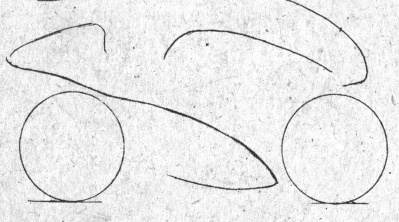

**STEP 2**

## STEP 3

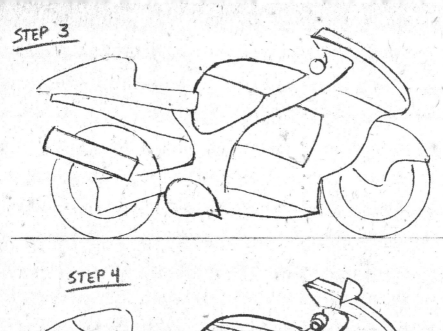

## STEP 4

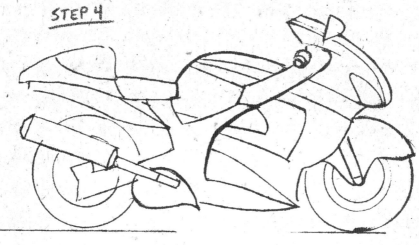

## FINAL!

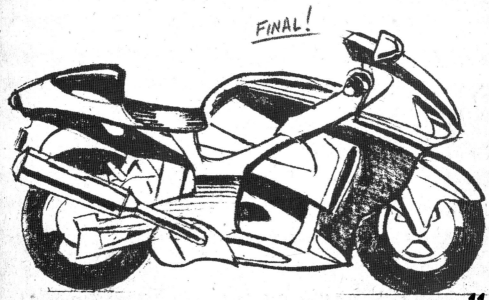

# THE DUAL RIDER

Sometimes it just isn't much fun to go for a ride by yourself. That's where the Dual Rider comes in. The roomy sidecar lets your best friend tag along for a ride on the open road.

When you're done drawing this bike, try adding a couple of friends going for a cruise!

STEP 1

STEP 2

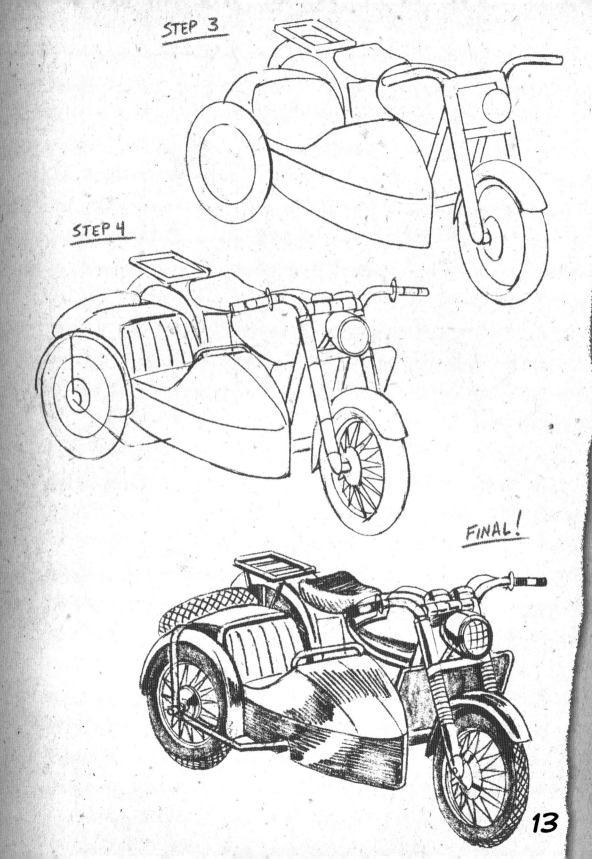

STEP 3

STEP 4

FINAL!

**13**

# SUPERBIKE RACER

Superbike racers are some of the most skilled motorcycle drivers in the world. They concentrate on every twist and turn while racing at incredible speeds. On tight turns, they often lean so low their knees scrape the ground!

## STEP 1

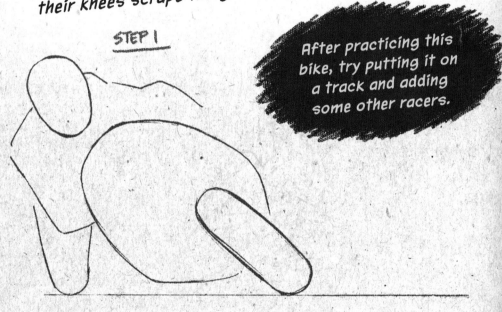

After practicing this bike, try putting it on a track and adding some other racers.

## STEP 2

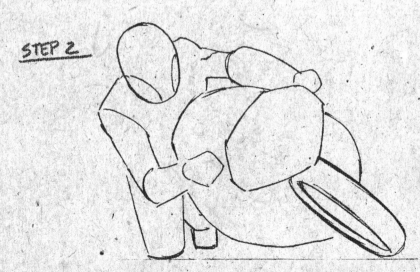

STEP 3

STEP 4

FINAL!

15

# THE SMITH-1000

The Smith-1000 combines the performance of a racing bike with the smooth ride of a large cruiser. It can also seat two people comfortably for those long cross-country rides. Give the Smith-1000 a try—you won't be sorry!

After drawing this bike, try it again using your own incredible paint designs!

STEP 1

STEP 2

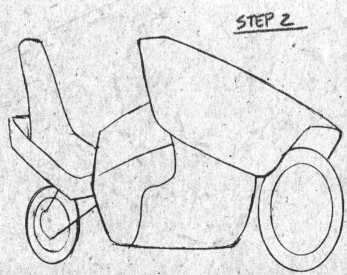

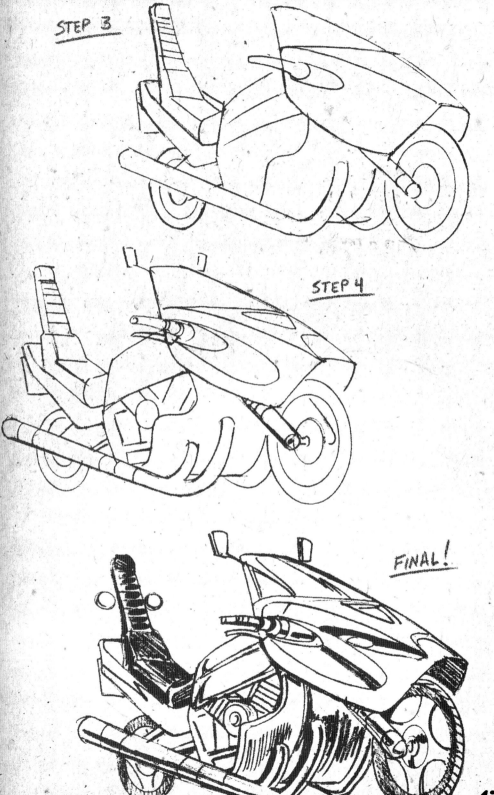

STEP 3

STEP 4

FINAL!

17

# THE BIKE OF TOMORROW

In the future, motorcycles may be much different from today's bikes. Streamlined bodies and reclining seats will make for a smooth, comfortable ride. A clear roof might help keep riders warm and dry on rainy days.

Try making your own bike of tomorrow! What kind of cool futuristic machines can you create?

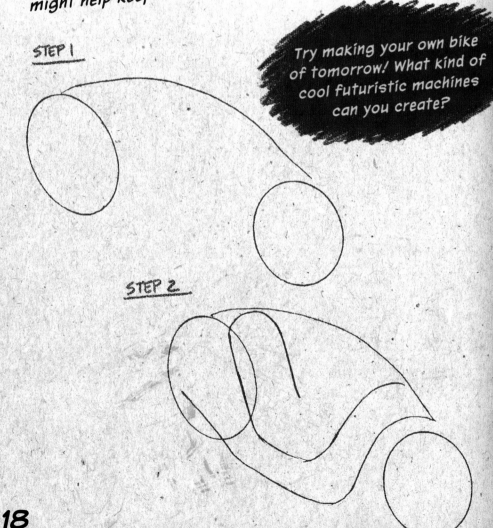

STEP 1

STEP 2

18

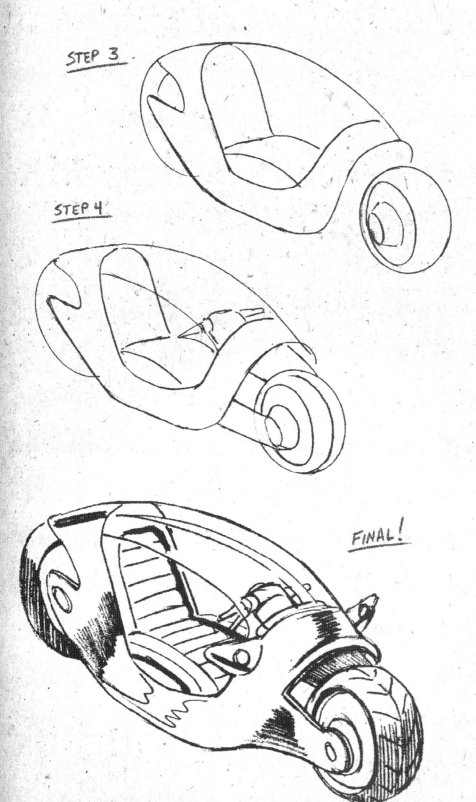

STEP 3

STEP 4

FINAL!

19

# THE DEMON

Engineers are already experimenting with new motorcycle designs and concepts. The Demon is one such experimental model. It's designed to go faster than anything else on the road, while giving the driver the smoothest possible ride.

Try making up your own cool paint job to give this bike some fun details!

STEP 1

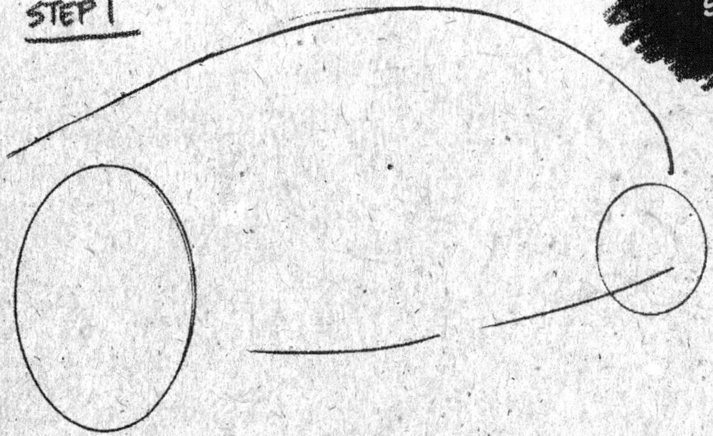

STEP 2

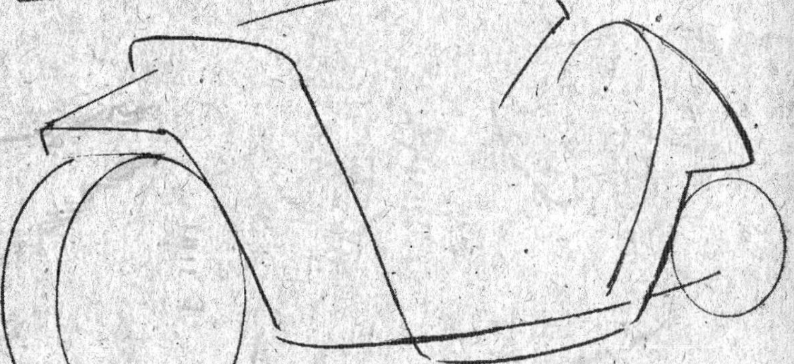

**STEP 3**

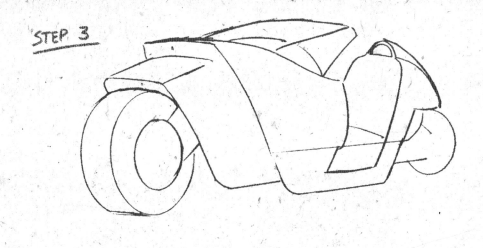

**STEP 4**

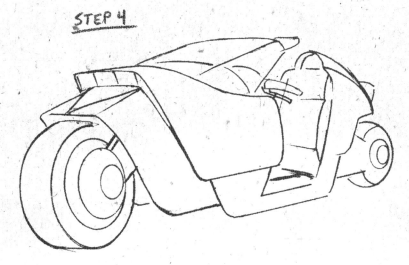

**FINAL!**

# FREESTYLIN'!

Motocross freestyle riders do all sorts of awesome, high-flying tricks. One of the most impressive is the Superman. Riders fly high in the air, then kick their feet out behind them while holding the seat or handlebars. Fans love to watch as riders perform these big-air stunts!

After finishing this drawing, try some other tricks. What sorts of crazy stunts can you make this rider do?

STEP 1

STEP 2

## STEP 3

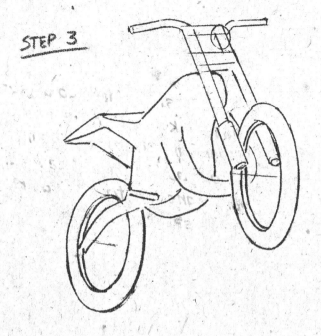

## STEP 4

TO FINISH THIS DRAWING,
TURN TO THE NEXT PAGE!

**23**

STEP 5

STEP 6

24

STEP 7

FINAL!

25

# THREE-WHEELIN"!

Three-wheelers are a slower type of motorcycle, but they have lots of personality. They don't tip over like regular bikes can, and they steer more like a car. But riders still love that feeling of freedom they get from driving on the open road.

After practicing this bike, try adding some mountains and trees. Nothing beats a ride through the countryside!

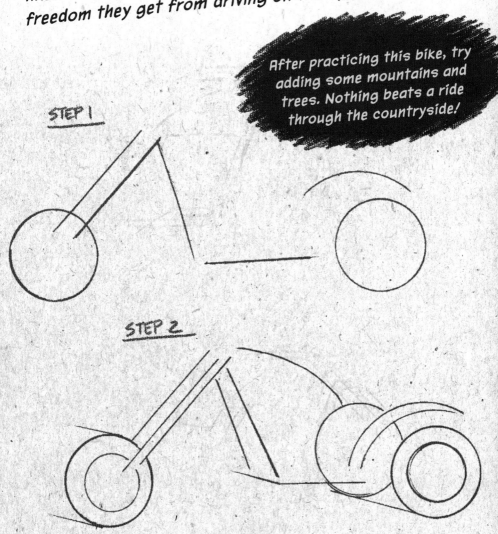

STEP 1

STEP 2

## STEP 3

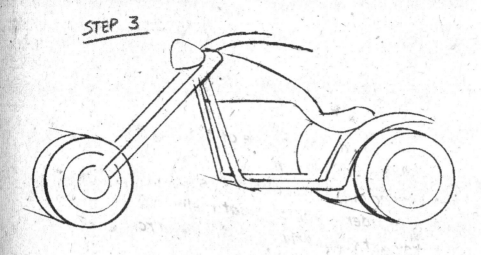

## STEP 4

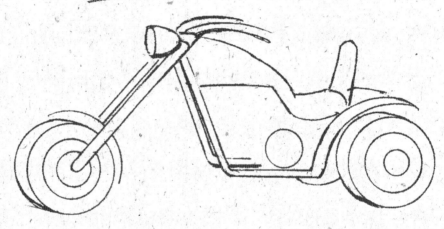

## STEP 5

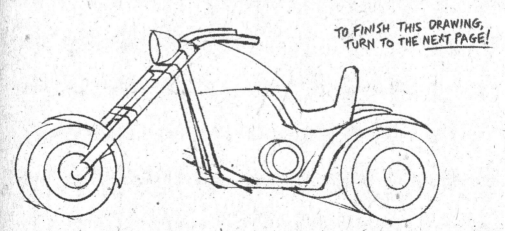

TO FINISH THIS DRAWING, TURN TO THE NEXT PAGE!

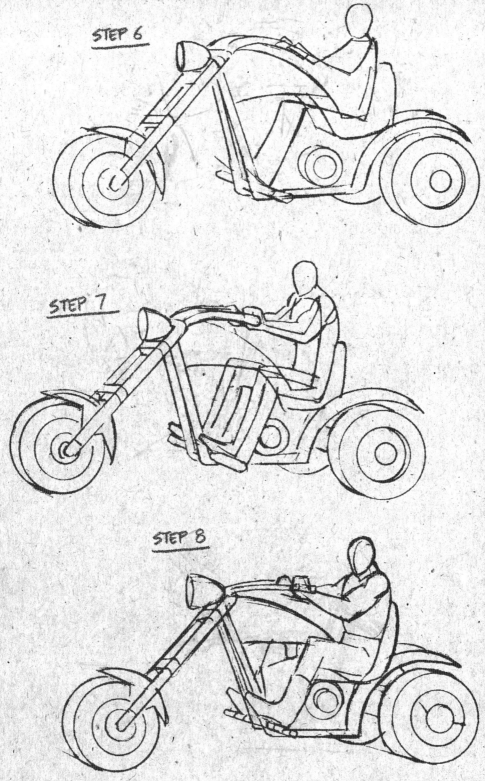

STEP 6

STEP 7

STEP 8

28

STEP 9

STEP 10

FINAL!

**29**

# GLOSSARY

**chrome** (KHROME)—a shiny metallic coating on a motorcycle part

**concept** (KON-sept)—an idea for a new way to build or create something

**customize** (KUHSS-tuh-mize)—to change a vehicle's appearance

**design** (di-ZINE)—to create the shape or style of something

**engineer** (en-juh-NIHR)—someone who is trained to design and build machines

**streamlined** (STREEM-lined)—designed to move easily and quickly through the air

**suspension** (suh-SPEN-shuhn)—a system of springs and shock absorbers that cushion a hard landing

**unique** (yoo-NEEK)—one of a kind

# READ MORE

**Barr, Steve.** *1–2–3 Draw Cartoon Trucks and Motorcycles: A Step by Step Guide.* 1–2–3 Draw. Columbus, N.C.: Peel Productions, 2005.

**Davis, Billy.** *How to Draw Motorcycles and Choppers.* New York: Scholastic, 2006.

**Walshe, Dermot.** *Mean Machines: How to Draw Cool Cars, Trucks and Motorcycles.* Cincinnati: Impact Books, 2007.

# INTERNET SITES

FactHound offers a safe, fun way to find Internet sites related to this book. All of the sites on FactHound have been researched by our staff.

Here's how:
1. Visit *www.facthound.com*
2. Choose your grade level.
3. Type in this book ID code **142960073X** for age-appropriate sites. You may also browse subjects by clicking on letters, or by clicking on pictures and words.
4. Click on the **Fetch It** button.

**FactHound will fetch the best sites for you!**

# INDEX